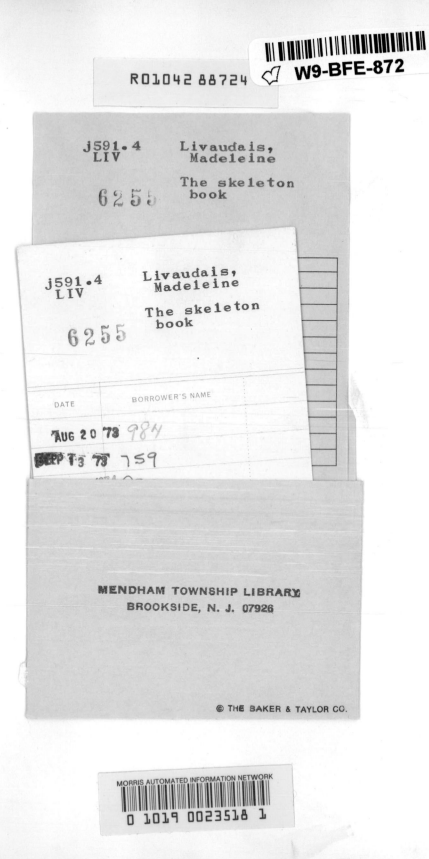

THE
SKELETON
BOOK
An Inside Look at Animals

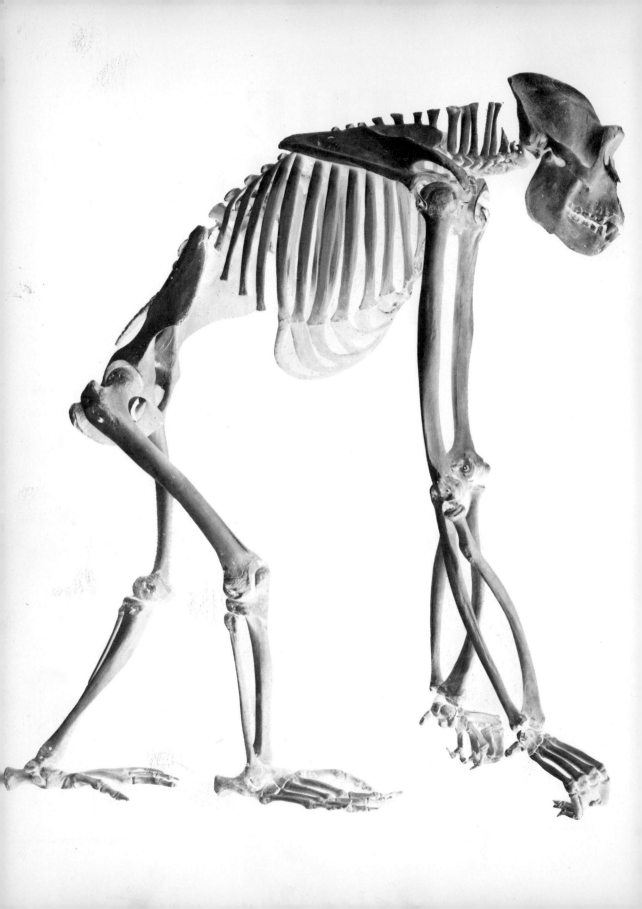

THE SKELETON BOOK

An Inside Look at Animals

By MADELEINE LIVAUDAIS
and ROBERT DUNNE

Walker & Company / New York

The Publisher wishes to thank Mr. Joseph Davis,

Scientific Assistant to the Director of the Bronx

Zoological Park, for reading the text of this book.

First published in the United States of America in 1972 by the Walker Publishing Company, Inc.

Published simultaneously in Canada by Fitzhenry & Whiteside, Limited, Toronto.

Trade ISBN: 0-8027-6125-9
Reinf. ISBN: 0-8027-6126-7

Library of Congress Catalog Card Number: 72-81381

Printed in the United States of America.

Book designed by Lena Fong Hor.

You are with a skeleton every day of your life. Your skeleton has 206 bones all linked together. Without a skeleton, you couldn't stand up. You couldn't sit up. You could only lie on the ground like a rag doll. Our skeletons support and give shape to our bodies. Our rib cage protects us, too. It protects such important organs as our heart and lungs.

Some animals have skeletons inside their bodies and some do not. Animals with inner skeletons are called vertebrates (VER-tuh-brayts) because their backbones, or spines, are made of bones called *vertebrae* (VER-tuh-bray). Animals without backbones are known as invertebrates (in-VER-tuh-brayts). Jellyfish, snails, and insects belong to this group.

Let's look at some animal skeletons. Can you guess what each one is before you read about it? Try to figure out how the skeletons are alike (do all have rib cages?) and how they are different (do all have leg bones?).

The skeleton of a snake is very simple. But there may be as many as 300 vertebrae in its backbone. Notice the pair of ribs attached to each vertebra except at the tail end. This particular snake has 160 pairs of ribs. Though this skeleton looks light, it is very strong. It supports many powerful muscles that help a snake glide over rocks and slither up trees.

See how the snake's lower jaws are separated at the front. A stretchy *ligament* connects these two bones in a live snake. This ligament allows the two parts of the jaw to move apart, enabling the snake to swallow an animal twice as wide as its own body.

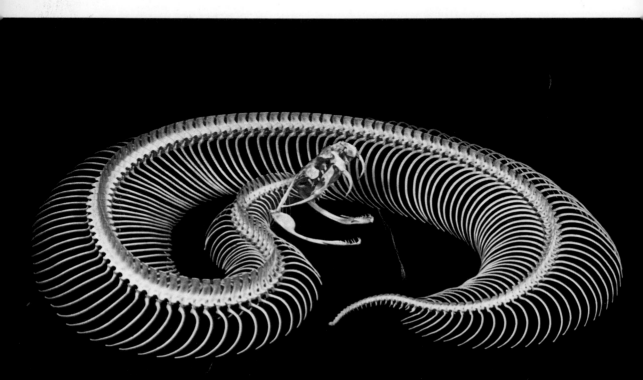

Look at how many bones there are in this skeleton of a fish. It has hundreds of bones. (That's why you have to be careful when eating fish. It's easy to swallow one or two.) Its skull alone is made up of over 100 bones. Your skull has only about 28.

There is a fin at the top. Notice how its bones come in between the bones of the backbone. Notice the bones of the other fins—one looks like a fan at the side of the head. Look at the fin bones below it and the fin bones near the tail. All these fins are used for steering and balancing the fish in the water. The tail fin is the most important since it helps to move the fish through the water.

This is the skeleton of a whale. It has the same fish-like shape of most animals that swim in the ocean. The long, heavy bones that stick up from the whale's vertebrae support large muscles that help to move the huge body through the seas.

In some types of whales (though not in this one), there are tiny hind leg bones. This has made scientists think that the whale was once an animal that lived on land. All whales have front limbs, though they are small and cannot be used for walking or holding up the body. The front limb bones support flippers which are used mainly for steering and balancing.

9

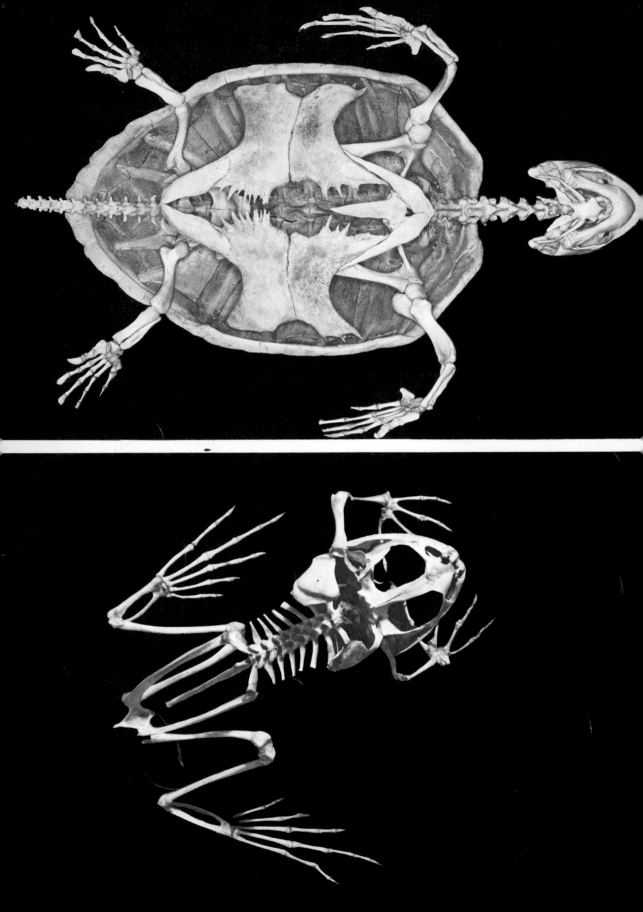

A turtle does not have a rib cage. It has a heavy lower shell that protects its heart, lungs, and stomach. The ribs are attached to its upper shell. Can you find them? Did you notice that most of the backbone of this turtle is also joined to the upper shell? If you have ever suddenly come upon a turtle, you know that it can draw its head inside its shell. This is because the neck vertebrae are not attached to the upper shell.

Did you find it hard to recognize a frog without its plump, slippery body? Or did the long, flat foot bones tell you at once to whom this skeleton belonged?

A frog rests with its hind legs doubled up under its body. In this position, it is always ready to jump. The frog's front leg bones are rather weak and serve mainly as "shock absorbers" when the frog lands from a jump. The bony eye sockets are quite large. Next time you have a chance to watch a frog, notice its bulging eyes. These eyes enable the frog to watch for enemies above, in front of, and to the sides of it.

A frog has only one vertebra in its neck. We have seven.

The beak on this skeleton tells you that it belongs to a bird.

You can see why a bird is able to fly. The large breastbone supports powerful wing muscles that move the bird through the air. Notice the many delicate wing bones. All of the bird's bones are hollow and light which helps it to stay up in the air. The skeletons of some birds may weigh less than their feathers!

Birds have more neck vertebrae than other animals with backbones. Swans may have as many as 24. This makes it possible for a bird to turn its head quickly and spot its enemies.

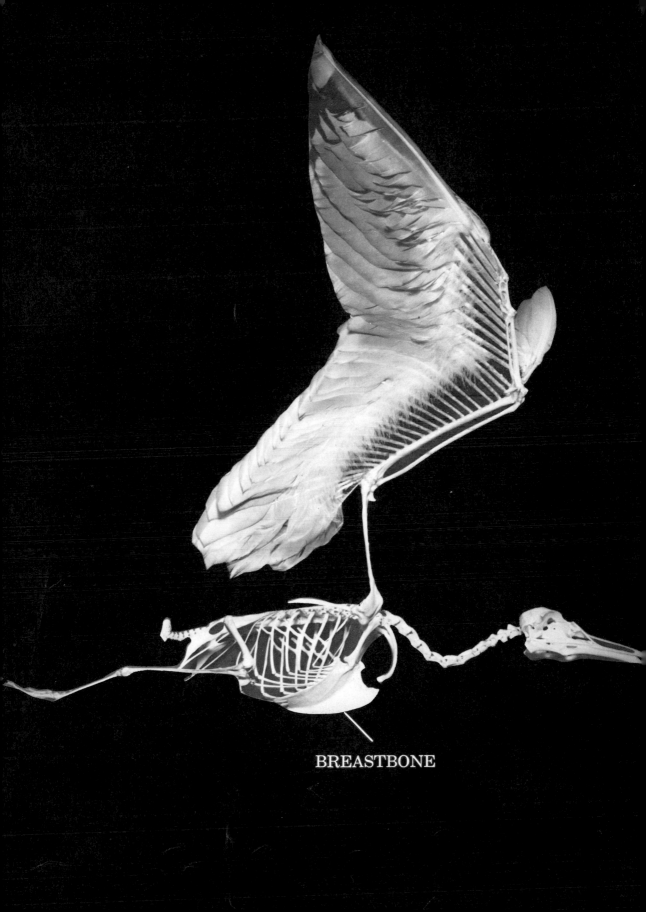

BREASTBONE

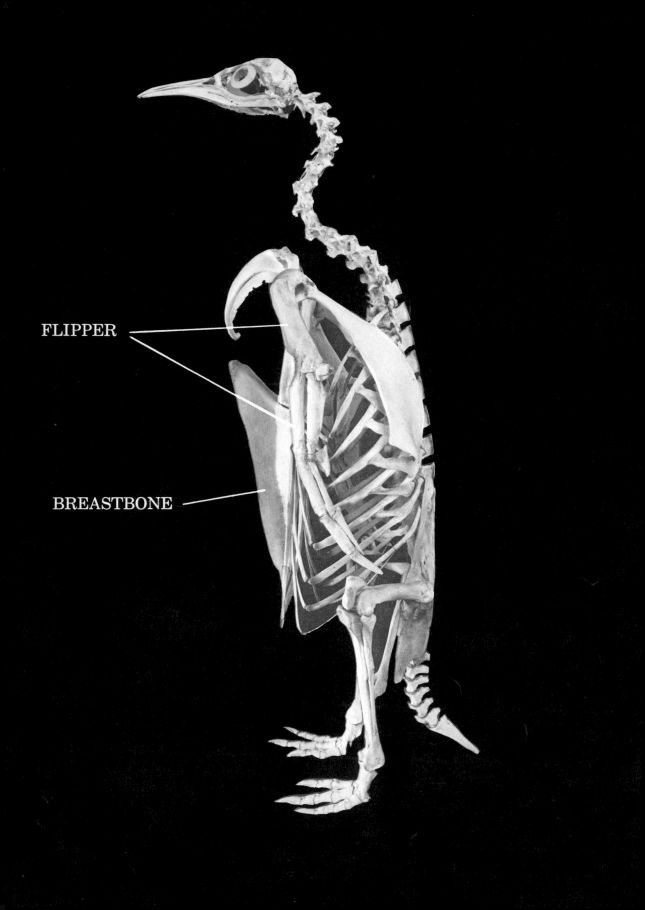

FLIPPER

BREASTBONE

A penguin is also a bird. Look at the beak. A penguin doesn't fly. Yet it has a large breastbone which supports powerful muscles. In this case, they are used for swimming instead of flying. A penguin has flippers, like a seal, instead of wings.

Notice the spine. There are many vertebrae in the neck. These enable the penguin to reach out quickly while swimming to catch fish in its beak. The penguin's lowest back vertebrae are joined together, making a strong support on which the bird rests. A penguin can "sit down" on its tail, as you do on a stool. This allows it to tilt back and lift the unfeathered soles of its feet off the Antarctic ice.

The bat, a flying mammal, has light, hollow bones like those of a bird. Notice the long, thin bones that support and stiffen the thin membranes that are the bat's wings. The bones are like our finger bones. Count them. The bat has five "fingers," just as we have. The hind toes end in sharp, strong claws. They hold onto a support when the bat hangs with its head downward.

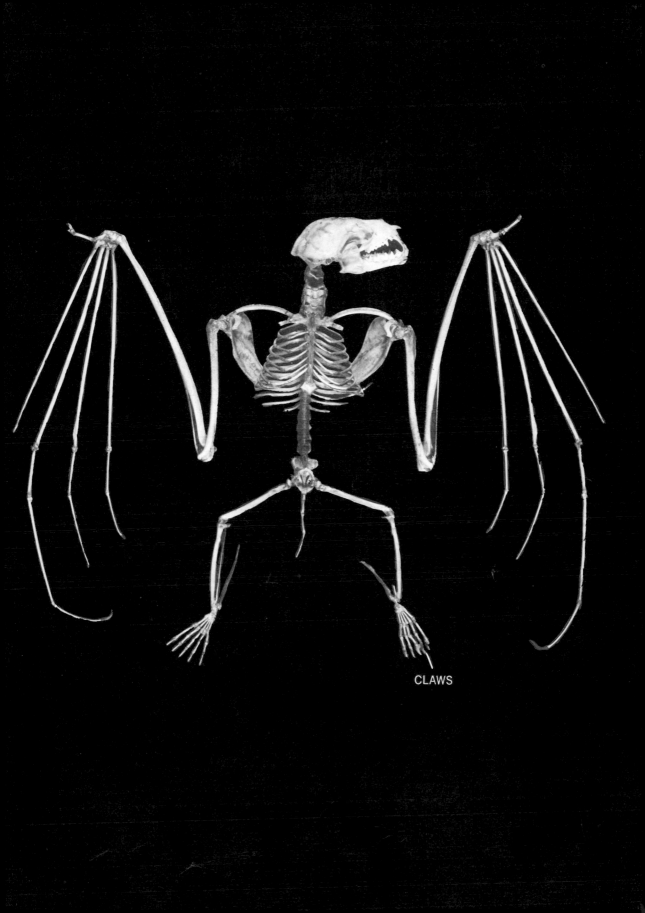

CLAWS

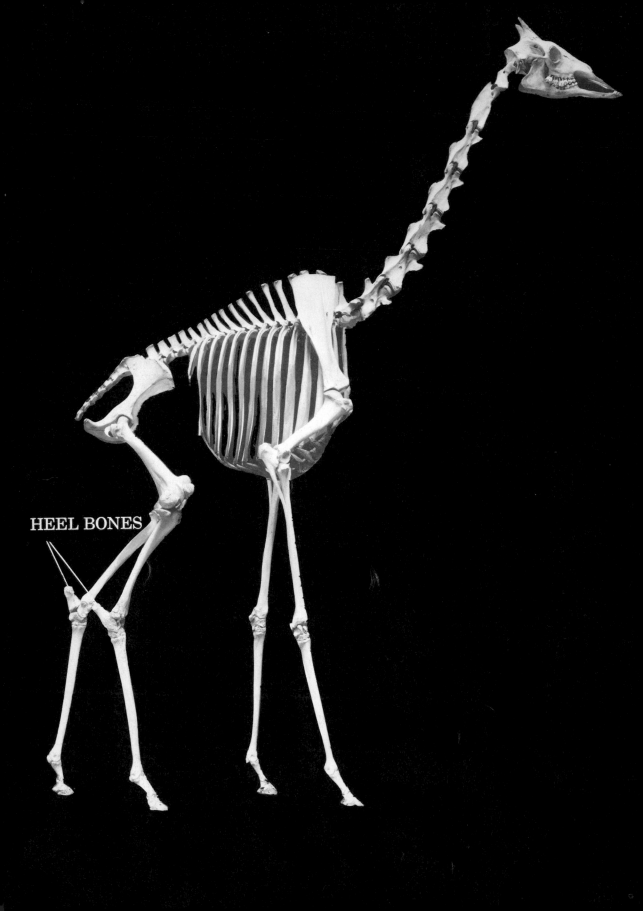

HEEL BONES

Although it has the longest neck in the animal world, the giraffe has only half as many neck vertebrae (7) as the tiny English sparrow (14). Can you count all seven? Its long neck makes it possible for it to reach the leaves and young stems at the tops of trees.

A giraffe lives on the plains of East Africa. It is able to run away from lions and leopards that try to attack it. Notice its long leg bones. Also notice that its foot bones are raised off the ground. The knobs sticking out from the backs of the giraffe's hind legs are its heel bones. This makes the giraffe's legs much longer and makes the giraffe a very fast runner. The giraffe runs on only two toes in each foot.

The horse is a runner, too. It has long leg bones and its feet are lifted off the ground. Look for the heel bones and ankle bones. Instead of running on two toes like the giraffe, it runs on only one toe.

The horse feeds on grass instead of leaves and stems like the giraffe. Its neck is just long enough to reach the ground. How many neck vertebrae do you count? Notice the large jaw that holds the big, flat teeth. These teeth grind and crush the tough grasses the horse eats.

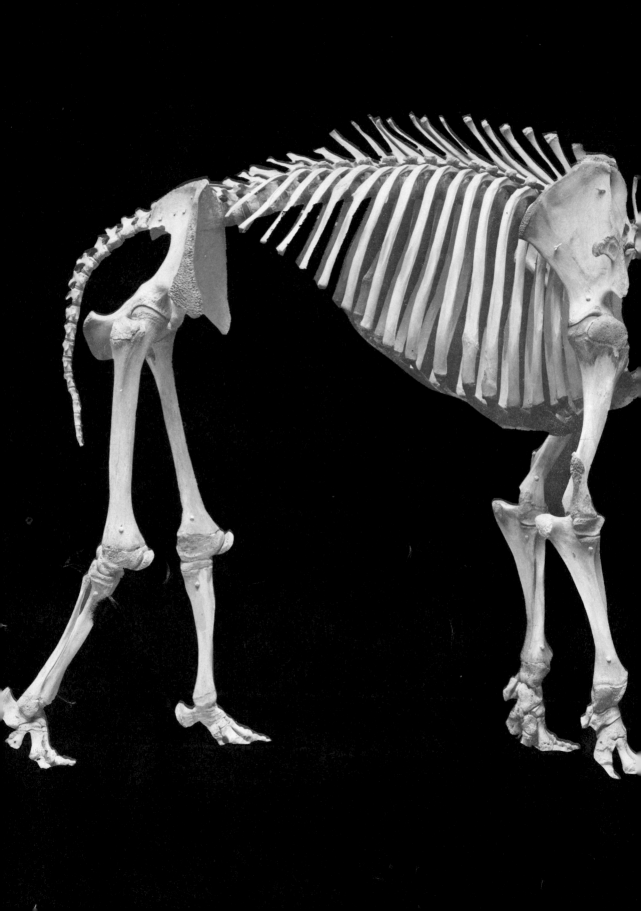

Of course you recognize this skeleton. This huge, bulky shape with tusks could only be the elephant. Can you figure out why you don't see its trunk?

Notice its long, heavy leg bones and its toe bones that are flat on the ground. The leg bones hold up its tremendous weight.

The elephant's famous tusks are really front teeth grown to enormous size. They are used in fighting and for digging up roots to eat. The rest of the teeth are flat-topped, which shows that an elephant eats plants. But elephants do not graze on grass like horses and they do not feed on the leaves at the tops of trees like giraffes. Instead, elephants use their trunks to carry leaves, twigs, and bark to their mouths. Notice how short the neck is compared to that of the giraffe or horse. Yet it has the same number of neck bones.

Do you recognize this skeleton? Here are some clues! It has many tail bones. It has big eye sockets in a small skull. It has two long, sharp teeth and it is the skeleton of an animal you might have as a pet.

This is a cat skeleton. The cat's long tail helps to balance it as it jumps from chair to table or walks along the top of a fence. The large eye sockets show that the cat has large eyes. They let in a lot of light and make it possible for the cat to hunt at night. A cat grabs, bites, and kills its prey with its sharp teeth. Pet cats eat mice and birds when no cat food is given to them.

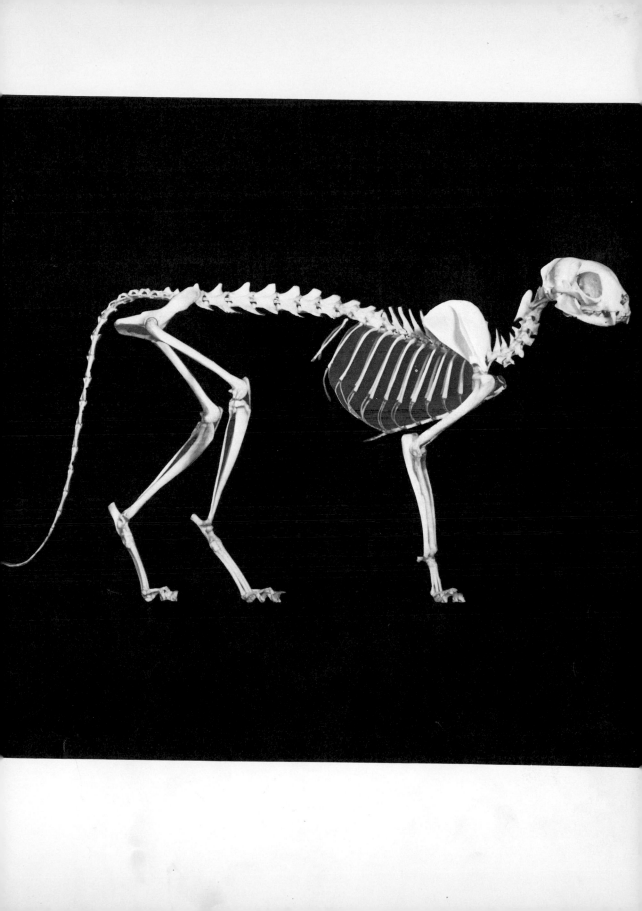

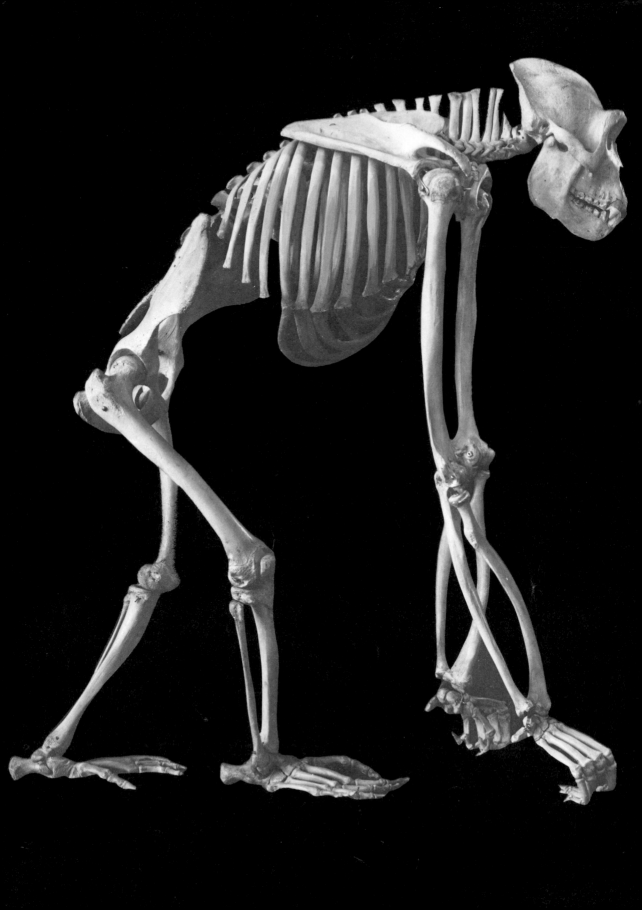

This skeleton looks like that of a man bending over. It is a gorilla skeleton. Gorillas walk hunched forward, partly resting their weight on their knuckles. Notice how much longer the arm bones are than the leg bones. Also notice how small the gorilla's hip bones are. Its hip bones do not carry as much weight as ours because a gorilla does not stand up straight. Most of the skull is taken up by the jaws and teeth.

Here is the skeleton of a human child. A human being can use his or her legs for running, but they are not nearly as fast as those of a horse or giraffe. A full-grown man can lift a heavy load, but he cannot begin to match the tremendous strength of a gorilla. He can swim, but not as well as a fish.

Are you surprised at the size of the skull? The human skull houses the largest brain in the animal kingdom. Our brains enable us to understand and solve problems. We also have two hands, each with four fingers and a thumb opposite them. These can grasp, hold, pull, push, twist, and turn. Our hands are able to use tools and put together anything from the simplest toy to the most complex machine.

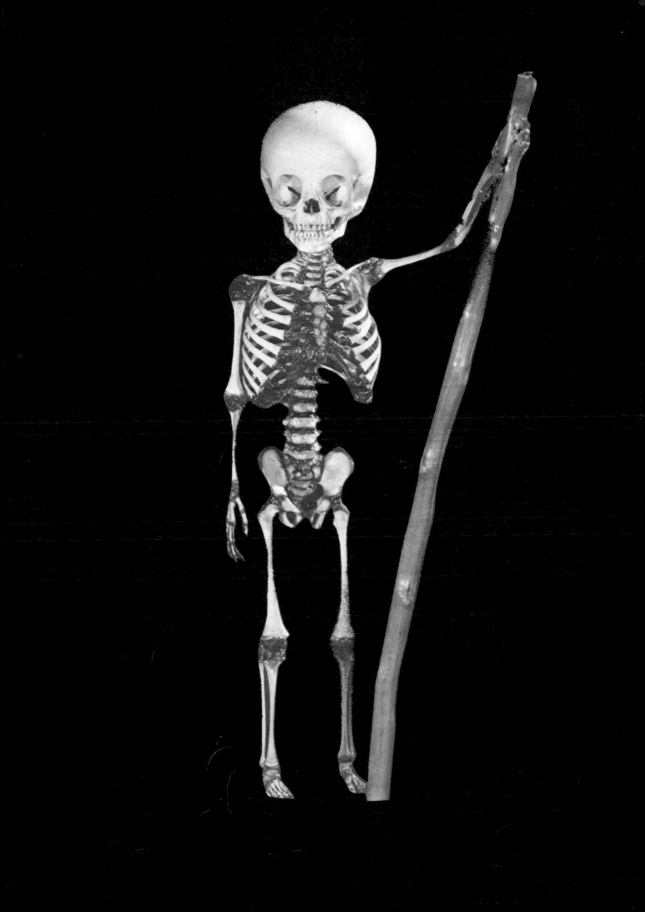

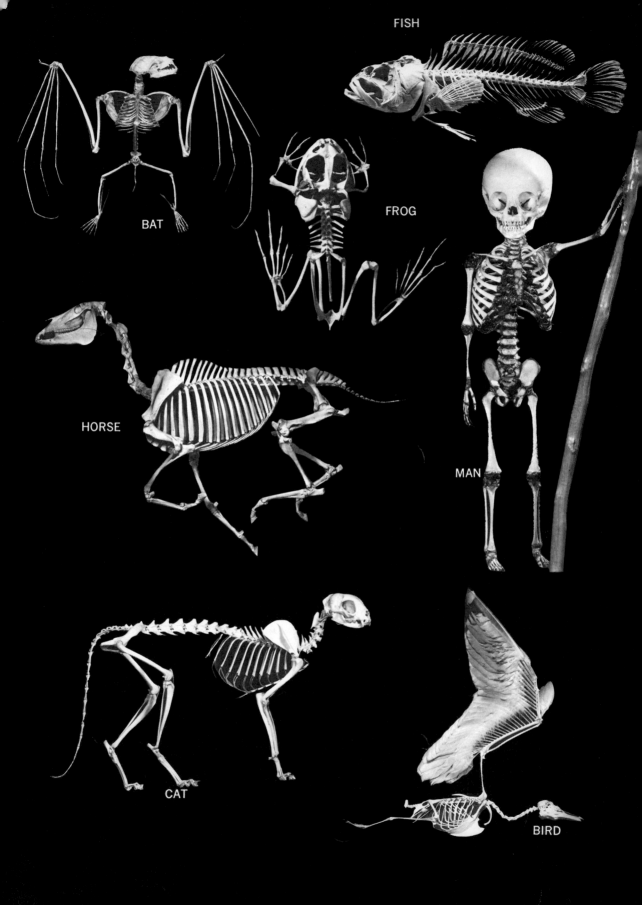

FISH

BAT

FROG

MAN

HORSE

CAT

BIRD

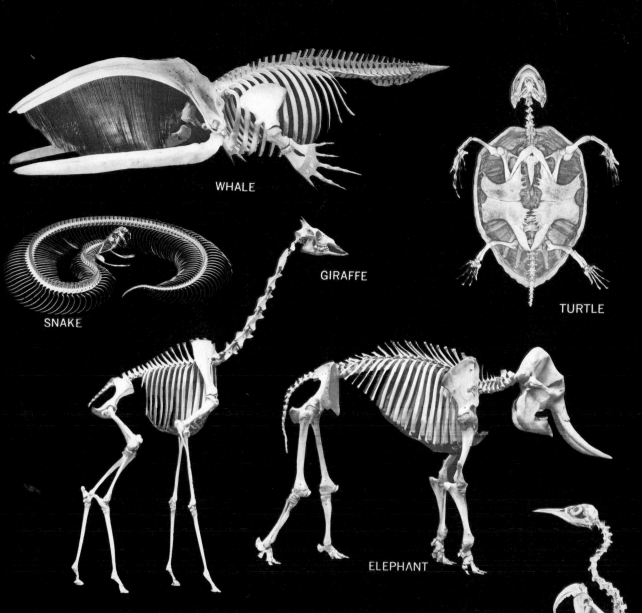

WHALE

TURTLE

SNAKE

GIRAFFE

ELEPHANT

PENGUIN

Look at all the skeletons together. You can see things that are alike and different. Notice that they all have a rib cage, skull, and backbone. Some have wing bones. Some have leg bones. Some have fin bones. All of these bones give you clues about how the animals live.

31

ACKNOWLEDGEMENTS

The publisher is grateful for permission to use the following photographs from the American Museum of Natural History: snake, p. 6; fish, p. 7; whale, pp. 8-9; turtle, p. 10; bird, p. 13; penguin, p. 14; bat, p. 17; horse, pp. 20-21; cat, p. 25; gorilla, p. 26; human, p. 29.

The publisher also wishes to thank Robert Dunne for the frog photo, p. 10, and the Field Museum of Natural History for the elephant photo, pp. 22-23, and the giraffe photo, p. 18.